TIMEPIECE

Jane Flanders

Timepiece

University of Pittsburgh Press

Published by the University of Pittsburgh Press, Pittsburgh, PA 15260
Copyright © 1988, Jane Flanders
All rights reserved
Feffer and Simons, Inc., London
Manufactured in the United States of America

Library of Congress Cataloging in Publication Data

Flanders, Jane. 1940–
    Timepiece / Jane Flanders.
        p.   cm. — (Pitt poetry series)
    ISBN 0-8229-3573-2.   ISBN 0-8229-5399-4 (pbk.)
    I. Title.   II. Series.
    PS3556.L347T5   1988
    811'.54—dc19   87-25191
                                                                CIP

Grateful acknowledgment is made to the following journals for permission to reprint poems that originally appeared in their pages: *Chelsea* ("Anatomy Theater: 1945," "The House that Fear Built: Warsaw, 1943," "In an Accelerated Time Frame," and "Milk Valley"); *Chowder Review* ("Dürer's Grasses"); *Commonweal* ("Care: The Hess Children, 1912" and "Van Gogh's Bed"); *5 AM* ("Checking the Camp" and "Spit"); *Image* ("Detail from the Assassination" and "Domesticity"); *Literary Review* ("The Fabulous Feats of Madame Houdini," "The Geography of Children," "Song of the Jaguar's Wife," and "You, Flying"); *Massachusetts Review* ("Ancestors" and "Spin the Bottle at Eleanor Hartle's"); *Mudfish* ("Impromptu," "Morning Glories," "Narcissus in Mid-December," and "Chiaroscuro"); *Nation* ("Flowering Privet"); *New England Review and Breadloaf Quarterly* ("Big Cars" and "Messenger"); *Poetry* ("Cloud Painter" and "Homage to Leonardo"); *Poetry Now* ("How I Began My Study of Leaves and Vines" and "Summing Up Mr. Cook"); *Prairie Schooner* ("Daughters," "Nightingales in America," and "Planting Onions"); *Shenandoah* ("Other Lives of the Romantics"); *West Branch* ("Headgear from the American Collection," "Twirling," "Falling," and "The Origin of Romanticism"); and *Xanadu: A Literary Journal* ("Screaming" and "Sleigh Ride: 1917").

"The Handbell Choir" is reprinted from *The American Scholar* (Winter 1988), vol. 57, no. 1. Copyright © 1988 by the author. "Shopping in Tuckahoe" was originally published in *Poetry Northwest* (Winter 1983–84), vol. 24, no. 4. "The House that Fear Built: Warsaw, 1943" appeared in *The Pushcart Prize, VIII.* "Cloud Painter" appeared in *The Pushcart Prize, X.* "Cloud Painter" and "The Geography of Children" appeared in the *Anthology of Magazine Verse & Yearbook of American Poetry*, 1985.

The publication of this book is supported by grants from the National Endowment for the Arts in Washington, D.C., a Federal agency, and the Pennsylvania Council on the Arts.

For Kate,
Dear First-born

Contents

Contents

II. World Without End

I

The Dangerous Moment

One minute before death, my iced foot touched
The lowest stair; and as it touched, life seemed
To pour in at the toes: I mounted up
As once fair Angels on a ladder flew
From the green turf to Heaven. "Holy Power,"
Cried I, approaching near the horned shrine,
"What am I that should so be saved from death?"

—John Keats, from "The Fall of Hyperion"

Falling

She says, "It's time,"
and runs her tongue
along his shoulder blade
in a new way.

He wonders dimly what "time" is,
another animal, perhaps.
On her lips the word hangs
spicy, overripe.

He snorts, shakes off
some heaviness that binds him.
The light is back
and the singing.

She wants him to follow,
takes his hand
and pulls him past
a lioness curled in the grass.

She will not even let him
stop to sniff
the ginger or snatch
a bite of guava.

Now they are running
through shade and blossom,
browsing herds, snakes
dangling liana-like.

The emptiness that comes
with light makes
him dizzy. An old ache
in his side starts up.

What is she saying now?
She has something to give him?
Little enough
but it will suffice.

Cloud Painter

—Suggested by the life and works of John Constable

At first, as you know, the sky is incidental—
a drape, a backdrop for trees and steeples.
Here an oak clutches a rock (already he works outdoors),
a wall buckles but does not break,
water pearls through a lock, a haywain trembles.

The pleasures of landscape are endless. What we see
around us should be enough.
Horizons are typically high and far away.

Still, clouds let us drift and remember. He is, after all,
a miller's son, used to trying
to read the future in the sky, seeing instead
ships, horses, instruments of flight.
Is that his mother's wash flapping on the line?
His schoolbook, smudged, illegible?

In this period the sky becomes significant.
Cloud forms are technically correct—mares' tails,
sheep-in-the-meadow, thunderheads.
You can almost tell which scenes have been interrupted
by summer showers.

Now his young wife dies.
His landscapes achieve belated success.
He is invited to join the Academy. I forget
whether he accepts or not.

In any case, the literal forms give way
to something spectral, nameless. His palette shrinks
to gray, blue, white—the colors of charity.
Horizons sink and fade,
trees draw back till they are little more than frames,
then they too disappear.

Finally the canvas itself begins to vibrate
with waning light,
as if the wind could paint.
And we too, at last, stare into a space
which tells us nothing,
except that the world can vanish along with our need for it.

The House that Fear Built: Warsaw, 1943

*"The purpose of poetry is to remind us
how difficult it is to remain just one person,
for our house is open, there are no keys in the doors."*
—Czeslaw Milosz

I am the boy with his hands raised over his head
in Warsaw.

I am the soldier whose rifle is trained
on the boy with his hands raised over his head
in Warsaw.

I am the woman with lowered gaze
who fears the soldier whose rifle is trained
on the boy with his hands raised over his head
in Warsaw.

I am the man in the overcoat
who loves the woman with lowered gaze
who fears the soldier whose rifle is trained
on the boy with his hands raised over his head
in Warsaw.

I am the stranger who photographs
the man in the overcoat
who loves the woman with lowered gaze
who fears the soldier whose rifle is trained
on the boy with his hands raised over his head
in Warsaw.

The crowd, of which I am each part, moves on
beneath my window, for I am the crone too
who shakes her sheets
over every street in the world
muttering
What's this? What's this?

Ancestors

—a daguerreotype

He's round-faced, going bald,
a placid man, slightly too smart
in his good clothes to be a farmer,
but that's what he is—
or a shopkeeper,

sitting up straight, while she,
with wild eyes, crooked smile,
slumps to one side
as if she's about to slide off her stool
or beat the photographer over the head
with her reticule.

They're dressed in black,
except for his vest, her collar
and cap with broad, trailing ties.
Someone has given them pink cheeks.
Their hands are in their laps.

Some anniversary made them sit so still
they slipped a century.
She thinks, "Should I have tied my cap?
This will never turn out. Hello,
out there, whoever you are." He's thinking,
"Fascinating, how these things work."

Messengers

—for Honey

If it is true that animals come from the gods
to teach us, that would explain
our reverence for the cat,
who stepped from the shrubbery as if from a bright cloud
into a circle of children. That would explain
why no one claimed her and we let her stay
though we thought we had no need.

It would be clear, then, why we stroke her,
why even her foolishness
enchants us—an *entrechat* out of the laundry hamper,
her passion for Brahms and string.
From staff of tail to opalescent eyes
she is telling us
to move with ease through manifestations of grace.

But then the toad, unearthed by the spade,
the pheasant that flew low over the yard,
shrieking as if from some dark cause,
the deer lying implacably still by the side of the road,
also are telling us.

Homage to Leonardo

"rerum cognoscere causas"—Virgil

knots, tendrils, cascades

O sweet complexity
yarn, ripples, roots
the endless folds of light

who has been more in love
with difficulty?

he undoes the body and
sees how it works
muscles, veins
a warrior's grimace

"Look at a woman as if
she were standing in a doorway
on a rainy day"

nothing too common
the penis erect
the anus, daisy-like
kidneys, the neck of an old man

no high road to the heart

a child clutches itself
in the womb, Vitruvian man
flails his manifold arms and legs
bodies rise from each other, flexed

la Gioconda to music

fantasy armor, seeds, stars
the deluge, maelstrom, holocaust
whatever is fugitive, far-fetched
an intricate coiffure

wouldst fight, wouldst fly
wouldst move the Arno from its course
wouldst stage the universe?

left-handed

In an Accelerated Time Frame

The jungle is full of green,
leafy snakes,
groping towards darkness.

Birds streak by. Orchids
go off with soft pops.
The sun beeps intermittently.

Debris rains down.
Your face emerges,
spilling its syllables.

And offshore,
the keening of whales rises
like birdsong.

Playing the Romantics

When I played the "Raindrop Prelude" Chopin began
to cough again, in a moldy cell in Spain.
It was summer in Pennsylvania. My sweaty thighs
stuck to the varnished bench. I played Schumann's
"Scenes from Childhood" while he paced the asylum
and Clara managed. By her door Brahms hovered
with another wistful ballade, an intermezzo.
All over Europe Liszt was seducing women.
Schubert was starving, Mendelssohn gasping for air.
They had it all—art, each other, and death.

Across the street a middle-aged redhead languished,
growing smaller and smaller until she was just a voice
on the phone to my mother. "Your daughter plays so
beautifully. . . . I used to play too." "After he
jilted her," Mother said, "she never again
walked." For her I raised the piano lid all
the way and executed "Liebestraum,"
"A Hungarian Rhapsody," "Rustle of Spring," till Mother
appeared and closed the lid with a small thud.

Stanley, the boy next door, kept running around
the block—an Olympics year—we were all inspired.
I composed poems and watched him turn the corner,
drifted from mirror to mirror to see if my nose
had stopped growing. Stanley was learning to drive.
He was a poet too and played the piano
faster and louder than I did. After a run
he often ended up on our side porch,
where I was reading what I considered the classics:
Anthony Adverse, The Fountainhead, Gone with the Wind.
Ashley was marrying Melanie. Scarlett and Rhett
were galloping through Atlanta. Atlanta was burning.
Stanley and I were both having trouble breathing.

Another neighbor, son of the haberdasher,
came back from New York playing "Malaguena."
He was going to be famous—Ivan Sherman.
I heard he lives in Baltimore. Stanley became
an orthodontist. Sometimes when I look at my daughter's
braces I think of him. On our old block
the windows are locked now, but in those days
they stood open wide. There were parades
and ox-roasts and dancing in the streets,
slow dancing in the feverous dark.

Spit

Mark 8:22–26

I could hear him spit on his hands.
That's how I knew what it was
when he touched my eyelids,
not a smelly potion
made from seeds and leaves
or some kind of oil like the others tried.
Nothing had worked.
Sooner raise a man from the dead
than make a blind one see.

It wasn't belief that did it.
I thought I was blind forever.
And when I heard him spit, I almost laughed.
How simple did he think I was?
People have always conned me or tried to.
Easy to fool a man with no eyes.
But this was the most bald-faced try ever.
Why didn't I strike his hands away?
Well, I didn't.
I was remembering how, when I was small,
my mother spit on the hem of her skirt
and wiped my dirty face.

People always ask me, what was it like,
to open my eyes and see for the first time
form, color, the things of this world.
Terrifying, I tell you.
For a moment I wanted the dark back,
hated those hands. "What do you see?"
he said. And because I was scared
I said, "I see trees walking."

He touched me again.
This time I raised my eyes to his
and saw there two little men staring back,
their mouths agape,
their hair and beards flying.
And then I did laugh.
No one had told me how funny things looked.
"Don't tell anyone," he said
(that must have been one of his jokes)
and turned away.

Well, that was that.
I heard later they got him on some charge
or other. There were strange tales
going around, but all I know is this:
I who was blind can see
and it was spit!

Sleigh Ride: 1917

—for Margaret Schroyer Hess, my mother

Remember the ride in the cutter to catch the train
from Milesburg home to Lewistown one winter
evening? You were three, your mother's death
was still four years away and light years off
your father's sudden collapse behind the desk,
your aunt's laborious breathing in the parlor.

Tucked in a rug between your father and grandpa
(he too had four years left) you blinked the flakes
from your eyes and smacked your lips. The train whistled.
Grandpa flicked his whip. Bells quickened.
The horse waltzed on through eddies of spun sugar.

In Grandma's kitchen the women were washing the dishes
and drying the dishes and putting the dishes away.
The dog dozed by the stove; the cats ate scraps.
Out back the chickens had already gone to roost
in the joy of their plump feathers. With time all this,
even the glittering fields, would vanish, but nothing
changed that Sunday night in Pennsylvania.

However, your grandpa, said to stun worms
before he hooked them, soon returned with a story
of how, when the cutter tipped at a bad curve,
Peggy flew like a bird beyond their grasp,
disappeared in a fluffy drift and was lifted out laughing.
Your hands were still in your new muff, little mother.
Trailing melted stars, you made the train.

Chiaroscuro

Derived from a sentence in *The Education
of a Gardener* by Russell Page: "It may
have been no longer possible even in the
great houses to find the footman who
would carry the wicker tables and chairs,
the chintz cushions and all the shining
silver paraphernalia of tea across the wide
lawns to the cedars' shade."

Every day it was harder to find the footman,
whom she depended upon to carry the wicker
tables and chairs, the chintz cushions and all
the shining silver paraphernalia of tea
across the wide lawns to the cedars' shade.

The others would have been quite content to sup
on the veranda, among the tubbed verbenas
and pots of petunias frothy as petticoats.
Tea was tea, wasn't it? Scones and tarts
and berries with thick cream, wherever one found it.
So if the footman vanished—no matter.

But it mattered to her. She had reached that certain age
when the cedars' chiaroscuro was necessary
as, indeed, was the footman, his lip curled
with a slight hint of malice, his eyes fixed
on her décolletage which the Baron no longer noticed.

She needed to listen for quick steps in the grass,
wanted someone to pick her up like a chintz cushion
and carry her down the esplanade, through
the maze to the parterre. "Love!" she'd murmur,
as he stared and placed before her the pink Spode
cups, fluted like cupids' lips. He was so

clever at thinking of new ways to hide—
among the yews, behind the stone lion,
espaliered like a peach against the wall.
She sat alone in the kiosk, trying to guess
where he would surface next, like a glossy lily,
but no one disturbed the lush, lingering dusk.

Flowering Privet

Left to itself, the hedge gradually rises
past roses, delphiniums, higher than doors and windows
till it reaches the trees and becomes a train of them,
bearing sparrows and warblers into summer.

Already the iris has lowered its sails.
Petals litter the grass and then sink into it.
And robins, which tumbled so lately from the nest
to tremble under the hemlocks are floating, drifting,
learning to track the worm's slow exodus.

Already the sun approaches its zenith. Soon
each day will again be less than the last.
Finally the hedge itself enters into the glory,
grows milky with stars whose fragrance thrills
the bees. Butterflies flicker like signal lights.

At night the opossum mounts a billowy frond
and sways as if bewitched. Voles twitter and
twitch at its base, nibbling crisp shoots.
And someone stepping out on the porch for a moment
into the scented shade, feels a gust of wind
on her face, as if she has just plunged into the wake
of something rushing past in the dark.

The Origin of Romanticism
—*a scene from* Der Freischütz

"I am the white dove," cries Agathe,
running across the stage in her white dress,
wreathed in the hermit's white roses.

Her lover has already raised his gun
to fire at white, whatever its blurred shape.

The bullet begins its song, swaying
from white to the dark Other. Both fall.
The lights go up. And the century ends
in a woods of cardboard and smoke.

But no, she lifts her head.
Her lover weeps. The distraught chorus revives.
We will live our long lives after all.

Sometimes it happens so.

How I Began My Study of Leaves and Vines

I lay in bed for days, eyes sealed,
while my skin simmered and popped like stew.
"Don't scratch!" they said. I was six or eight,
almost old enough not to. Mostly I did
in my sleep, smearing the sheets with blood.

When my eyes came unstuck, I could see
no one except my parents would ever love me.
Later, my face clearer than my fate,
Dad walked me down a country lane and said,
"This is poison ivy. Watch out!"

Its glossy, triple tongues wagged in the breeze,
licking trunks and posts with vicious green.
I stood there a long time, just out of reach.
So, at last, do we come to know our enemies.
We heal and burn. Heal and burn.

Care: The Hess Children, 1912

There is a woman behind this photograph, ironing
the girls' white dresses, flounce by flounce, braiding
their hair, tugging at bows.
                              She arranges them all
in the yard under a tree, placing the baby
where one of the girls can catch him if he moves
beyond the frame.
                   And now she is standing behind
the photographer, so they will all look this way,
giving back her patient stare.
                                She is waiting
for boys to go off to war, for girls to get married.
Some will; some won't.
                        A big girl fidgets. The baby
plays with his toes. A little girl grins.
The children are handsome.
                            They are more than that.
But all she can think of now is immaculate dresses,
how she must save them before they are stained by the grass.

Spin the Bottle at Eleanor Hartle's

Milk makes you grow.
At every meal I get a big glass of it.
My parents eat and leave the table but I
must stay till the milk is gone. Maybe I drink it.
Often, however, I pour it down the drain
or into the bushes by the back door or even,
once, into a wastebasket, which leaks.
I do grow.

When I'm almost eight I go
to Eleanor Hartle's party, an impromptu
affair, for which I'm overdressed. Eleanor's
big brother and two of his friends are there.
They're rangy and good at sports (so's she)
but not so good at dropping clothespins into
a bottle. I'm winning at that, when someone
abruptly turns the bottle on its side
and sets it spinning.

A circle forms. We crouch
like cavemen over knucklebones. Late light
illuminates our skin. Surely some old
master must have thought of thinning his paint
with milk, to achieve this soft, particular glow.
Each time the bottle stops a pair goes off
and trudges back, blushing, vaunting, grinning.
Rosalie has to kiss Eleanor's brother.
I, Miss Muffet, will never kiss anyone,
even though someone has finally set the bottle
spinning for me.

The milk it contained has long
been drunk and cream in its slender neck thriftily
skimmed off. Now at the edge of town cows
gather to be relieved of more, and our mothers
are putting the shining empties out to be

22

retrieved by those who come before we wake.
The spinning bottle points to chairs, a cake,
the dog, snoring by the door, the four corners
of the room, the globe, sending us out to school,
to work, to get married. In a few seconds that last
forever it spins as we'll spin ourselves, till the world
tilts and we stagger off with our funny dreams.

✣

And who was it I had to kiss, in the dim
hall beside the stairs? Skinny Eleanor!
who became, with time, surprisingly full-breasted.
She took off her glasses and squinted at me. "Come on,"
she whispered, as if speaking of life itself,
"It won't hurt." And it didn't. Not then.
Her lips, beneath a thin mustache of milk,
were warm and sweet.

Screaming

While you were being born, I screamed
as if about to burst. And once,
as your father and I trudged through a woods,
I screamed when a snake rose up beside him,
though it was harmless as garden hose.

The sounds I made seemed scarcely human,
echoes of animal confrontations, sirens,
Munch's shriek, Ivan Ilyich's "O" as he
careened towards death on his chaise lounge.

As we fall earthward the music of fear
accompanies us.
Your first sound too was a scream,
after you had been awkwardly worked from the womb,
cut loose, and held aloft.

You, Flying

—for Steve

I am watching you fly
with your arms flung wide
you are lying on air like Superman—you
my middle-aged love—are floating, gliding
your arms are spread, you are
wearing your glasses and looking down
as if at a page containing your life
chrysanthemums mask the picket fence
a few red leaves are waving you on
in your old clothes and flying shoes

Your pockets contain a pen knife
handkerchief, keys, small change
I will have reason to ponder these later
the worn belt, the hole in the sock
but I'm not thinking of anything now
I'm not thinking that if I run
very fast I might somehow prepare the ground
for you, I'm not thinking
I might have held the ladder firm
while the treetop crashed

I'll think of everything sooner or later
and wonder if I could have kept
you in the air and wonder
why we didn't call to each other
we don't call, we are silent
the children are not at home
it is Saturday morning, the neighbors are still
asleep, and we are intent
on the thing at hand, you are flying
and I am watching you

The Handbell Choir

Twelve children, twelve gray geese in starched
collars, file onstage. Like their bells,
which are set out buffet-style on a long table,
they are graduated. The gym, with its folding chairs
and stale air, seems wrong;
they belong in a cloister or small pond.

The director, also in gray, appears.
They will play "Geese . . ." no, "Sheep May Safely Graze,"
in honor of Bach's three hundredth birthday.
Her raised hand, their rapt stance quiet us,
who suddenly seem to be listening
for a rush of wings. But the advent
is simply that of a sweet chord.

With a flick of the wrist, each bell is rung
then silenced on the breast. No hurry.
They take all the repeats,
arms rising and falling stiffly, like clockwork
hammers sounding over the roofs of Eisenach
on a March day for the baptism of the infant
Johann Sebastian. We think of sheep and lambs
in spitting snow. The church is clammy, water cold
on a baby's head, he cries a bit—
another miraculous, ordinary birth.

Having happened, the past is safe.
This is the dangerous moment, the melody passed
from hand to hand. Tirelessly, ancient-eyed,
they raise their bells as if in blessing, yes,
someone here, now, is blessing us.

II

World Without End

"If the doors of perception were cleansed every thing would appear to man as it is, infinite."
—William Blake, from *The Marriage of Heaven and Hell*

Parlor Organ

Have we moved heaven and earth
or was it just a parlor organ
we urged over the threshold and up the steps?
Surely upon these parapets
ceramic angels used to stroll
among the scrolls and finials, looking down
on tiny porches where assorted ancients perched
in their daguerreotypes and light dawned
from a glass globe rife with roses.

A mirror over the music rack radiates bemusement—
could this be us among the fruit and flowers,
accompanied by time's ticking obelisk?
We unearth from behind the rack
a six-year warranty (1905) plus Getze's
*New and Improved School for the Parlor Organ
including Numerous Voluntaries* (1876).

Within this wedding-cake-shaped cosmos (chocolate)
swells, in voices both *humana* and *celeste,*
a wheezy version of "Blest Be the Tie that Binds,"
while ghostly hands reach round us
pressing extra keys.
"Push the treadles down *all the way,*"
pleads Getze, "or else a jerking sound is produced
which is very disagreeable."

We have much to learn, Mr. Getze,
(is that you playing the octaves?)
about treadles, stops, "jerking sounds,"
those "jarring noises" you also mention,
and the baroque ties that bind us
to everything we thought we left behind.

Dürer's Grasses

After the Virgin Birth and the Apocalypse
there came a suet-pudding day
with Agnes scolding in the yard.
There must be times like this
when the spirit sleeps or walks abroad
as he did, out of the city.

A blur of wings startled him—grasshoppers.
An old woman passed with a wen on her lip.
He thought about God, who allows old women
their sorrows. If he had a dog
he would whistle now and the dog would come,
feckless, gay, to lick his hand.

After a while he lay down.
The sky was made of Venetian rags.
Rain would come later and rinse away the heat.
The wind began a simple song,
like his mother sang to the little ones.
A young man sets out to discover the world.
A girl doffs her disguise.
The greenest grass reveals the grave.

There is something about the earth
that makes a man want to return to it—
dust gone wild in its longing to be
timothy, yarrow, daisy, dandelion.

He dug his fingers into the loam
and ripped up a large piece of turf.
He would carry it home and make of it
what he could; leaves, stems, dirt and all,
roots, pebbles. There would be mud
on the kitchen floor. Agnes would say,
"What's that?" And he would answer,
"An angel's wing. A map of Nuremberg.
A small, dusty star."

Shopping in Tuckahoe

One could spend years in this parking lot
waiting for a daughter to find just the right
pair of jeans. From time to time I slip the meter
its nickel fix. Across the street in Epstein's
basement, shoppers pick their way through bins
of clothes made tempting by the words "marked down."
We have replaced making things with looking for them.

My mood is such I almost miss what's happening next door,
where a weedy lot is conducting its own
January clearance with giveaways galore—
millions of seeds, husks, vines, bare sepals
glinting like cruisewear in the cold sun.
"Come in," says the wind. "We love your pale hair
and skin, the fine lines on your brow."

The shades of choice are bone and dust, everything
starched, rustling like taffeta, brushing against me
with offers of free samples—thorns, burrs, fluff,
twigs stripped of fussy flowers.
Greedy as any bargain hunter, I gather them in,
till my arms are filled with the residue of plenty.

By the time my daughter reappears, trailing her scarves
of pink and green, she will be old enough
to drive home alone. I have left the keys for her.
She'll never spot me standing here like a winter bouquet
with my straw shield, my helmet of seeds and sparrows.

Planting Onions

It is right
that I fall to my knees
on this damp, stony cake,
that I bend my back
and bow my head.

Sun warms my shoulders,
the nape of my neck,
and the air is tangy with rot.
Bulbs rustle like spirits
in their sack.

I bury each one
a trowel's width under.
May they take hold,
rising green in time
to help us weep and live.

Headgear from the American Collection

Pennsylvania, mid-twentieth century

My father's fedora, cocked like Clark's,
tipped to ladies.
Under the crown his hair seemed to be growing back
over the bald spot.

Methodist women's Easter bonnets, quivering
with fruit and flowers
and small birds impaled on hat pins
while flying towards Paradise.

A Brownie beanie, to cover my bean.

My aunts' starched, organdy caps, pleated,
tied under the chin, worn everywhere except to bed.
Outdoors they wore black gabardine bonnets
and were still beautiful.

The hot, windy cone my mother wore at the beauty parlor.

My uncles' black hats with broad brims.
Put one on and speak with authority.

Cousin Howard's golf cap. He was Scotch-Irish.
Other side of the family.

The air-raid helmet from the attic.

Davy Crockett caps with real coontails
that made my brothers' crew cuts lie down flat.

The scarves we tied under our chins. Sailors.
Berets. Veils. Pinwheels.
Whatever was needed for love, propriety, defense.

When we put on our hats we stood tall.
We had to be reckoned with.
Our spirits did not escape into the blue
unruly stratosphere.

33

Morning Glories

The morning glories start their trip to the sky
out of dust under the eaves, from stony ground
with little to offer, presenting themselves as small
sets of mauve mittens which then unravel
and knit again into hearts, green hearts.

They want to climb the trellis beside the house,
though a few prefer to strangle the marigolds
or wreathe the downspout. Oh, they make mistakes.
Some enter darkness under the porch, get lost
in spidery trash and have to be forced back.

Set right, they twirl on to the next
regret, that the trellis is interrupted, nothing
to grab and make your own, nothing. They reach
and find only each other, till hands appear
to hook them firmly into the final grid.

Vines thicken, the climb becomes a dance.
Like young goats, they sprout tender horns.
Above them stretches the roof, a shadeless, vast
bourn. And if, come morning, the sun shines,
their first cerulean notes may waken us.

Other Lives of the Romantics

1808   Wordsworth dies from fall while hiking in Scotland.

1811   Blake takes concubine.

1818   Byron teaches Shelley to swim.

1819   Shelley has affair (probably platonic) with Miss X. Mary returns to England.

1820   Blake takes second concubine.

1822   Shelley, exhausted after boating mishap, contracts pneumonia. Mary returns to Italy.

1823   Keats marries Fanny Brawne, establishes apothecary practice in Hampstead.

1824   Blake teaches concubines to read, write, color engravings.

1825   Shelley has affair (possibly platonic) with Mme. Y. Mary returns to England.

1826   Byron reunited with Lady Byron; disposes of 8 horses, a mule, 11 dogs, a macaw, 3 peacocks, a monkey, a lamb, and a tyger.

1827   Blake ascends to Heaven.

1830   Coleridge completes "Kubla Khan."

1831   Shelley shows signs of consumption. Mary returns to Italy.

1833   Coleridge completes "Cristabel." Leigh Hunt moves to Chicago and founds *Poetry* magazine.

1834   Coleridge dies after critics pan "Cristabel."

1839   Keats discovers anesthesia.

1840   Shelley dies while leading uprising of croupiers in Monaco.

1845   Keats operates on Byron's Achilles tendon, corrects lifelong limp.

1857   Byron completes "Don Juan" (199 cantos), embraces Calvinism.

1862   Keats dies from drug overdose.

1883   Byron dies in sleep at age 95; posthumous publication of his "Ecclesiastical Sonnets."

Twirling

Spring and the girls are twirling batons,
learning *beginnings* and *endings,*
aerials, swings, salutes, capers, wraps.
Everywhere batons spin and bounce.
The girls' wrists ache. They have chapped
hands, sore calves and thighs.
Twirling drives them to bed early.

Beth Skudder and Mary Lou Ravese,
captains of the varsity twirling team,
send messages: "Use imagination!
It's always nice to see something new."

They will progress with time from *butterflies*
to *tea cup slides* and *rainbow reverses,*
set their wands on fire,
become the hubs of chancy wheels.

In Beth Skudder's dream, she does the
heliocopter on the gym roof,
creating a field of force no one can enter.
Soon she begins to rise, still twirling,
over the track, the trees, the parking lot.

She's a space probe, asking what's out there,
waving goodbye to the twirlers below,
whose bodies shimmer, then dim, like lights
from a little town quickly passed over.

Impromptu

When did you first learn air's secret?

It has been here all along,
fluffing up the world,
making your chest rise and fall,
blowing right through you.

You too can float or push the air aside
like a beaded curtain
closing perpetually after you.

Only in fairy tales do you run up against
invisible walls of air, solid as glass,
spiteful, treacherous.

There is no magic in air. Only good feeling.

Say it: fresh air, pure air,
mountain air, night
air, full of fragrance and Schubert's gaiety.

It makes you want to smile too,
it is so simple.

It makes you wonder about everything else
you never believed in.

Daughters

Doors bang
a bud breaks and shows us its heart
spring is always like this

Once the earth cracked and a girl slipped in
along with a herd of swine
imagine that rain of bodies in the dark

Or was she a pig-girl
a troll child with kinky tail
perhaps it has nothing to do with you and me

It was the edge of a flower
from which she fell
into a bearded mouth breathing garlic and dust

She had been gathering daisies
she had been thinking of something else
she had been fixing her hair in a new way

O, this is our story after all
they move so lightly away
trailing garlands of song

Song of the Jaguar's Wife

My husband walks abroad and the earth grows still.
He circles the clearings and takes what he pleases.
His eyes are torches. His claws are knives.
His teeth shine from the bones of his enemies.
He wears a cloak of dead men's kisses.

Ai-ya, ai-ya, sisters of stick and hoe,
    weep, but not for me.

My husband rides the wind. He leaps from cloud to cloud.
He drinks from the eye of the storm, yet
His touch is soft as a boy's cheek.
His voice is soothing as wild honey.
He carries me into the cave of forgetfulness.

Ai-ya, ai-ya, sisters of stick and hoe,
    weep, but not for me.

I will never grow old scratching in dirt.
My skin is smooth as the river bank,
My mouth unpinched from feuds and petty sorrows.
I take my ease in the tall grass.
In the tall, singing grass I wait for him.

Ai-ya, ai-ya, sisters of stick and hoe,
    weep, but not for me.

I will never come back to huts and the stink
Of small fires, for I have been given a flame
That burns in the loins and smokes the soul
Till it is strong and of use to no one—to itself only,
Able to live alone when the god departs.

Ai-ya, ai-ya, sisters of stick and hoe,
    weep, but not for me.

The Geography of Children

*"I remember having seen somewhere a
geography text which began thus: 'What
is the world? It is a cardboard globe.'
Such precisely is the geography of
children."* — Jean-Jacques Rousseau,
from Emile

Geography is the room at the top of the stairs
where Mr. Haugh reigns, waving a yardstick —
first stop on the rise to seventh grade.
He sizes us up with bulging eyes, rattles
his keychain. Already he knows, and so do we,
who'll make trouble, which girls he'll tease,
which boy will taste his simmering rage.

Flexing his gauge he begins the long slog
over a cardboard sea, holding up for us
strange creatures who eat dogs or scar
themselves or stalk their prey with poisoned darts.
Meanwhile Carl Rudy perfects the art
of rolling his eyes back in his head like Caesar.
Carolyn Adams and Susie Breidenthal
agree they won't walk to school with me anymore.

"This is the Amazon," says Mr. Haugh.
We chew paper, toy with the rubber bands
on our new braces, till they pop or fly off
like tropical bees. He crosses the equator
and stalks north along the seventy-eighth
meridian. We study each other's necks and knees,
the clock, the cracks, the scratches on our desks
which truly, truly show us the way.

Nightingales in America

The older women were Sunbeams and I guess we
were Cherubs or Lambs but our mothers were Nightingales.
Sunday mornings they prayed and sang in a niche
of the Methodist Church. They studied the sorrows of Jesus
and all who suffered in places like Abyssinia,
where there was still so much to be done.
There was much to be done everywhere, of course—
bake sales, suppers, altars, the homely chores
women were made for. Once a year, however,
they paused in their good works and took us all
to Cold Spring Park. After we skidded around
the roller rink maybe a million times,
seesawed, swang, got skinned and bitten, skittered
through poison ivy, fell in the creek, rode
the little train and ate our fill we lay back
blissfully in the grass and watched our blessed
mothers, their wings suddenly tinged with gold,
wheel overhead in the shape of a cross, singing
a wistful hymn we never could remember.

Detail from the Assassination

The evening is detained by arabesques.
In this faint light, which are foxes, which deer?
Heron and cock fly a collision course
but do not collide. Blue
loons court in suspended flight.

Overhead, angels in red and green,
their wings forking
into the world's parameter, define
a gaudy Paradise—gold chords,
gold plates of sweets among the clouds.

Silence has long out-distanced
quick feet on the stairs,
a cry, spilled wine.
But see, through the open door, dark sky,
the sanguine persistence of hollyhocks.

The Fabulous Feats of Madame Houdini

I was the loose change that rolled away.
I was youth, your own, that flooded you briefly
with cunning—the knife that slipped
and then ran off
with the butcher but now he's forgotten me.

On foggy nights I was the white
line, the one you clung to.
I was the pin you dropped
that came back to stab you from love, not malice.
Love too has its tricks, knows how
to hold its breath,
escape from locked trunks.

Mine was a natural talent, developed
by unraveling Mother's crocheting, teasing
the knots from my shoes. At school
I escaped in the pages of books.
As a bride I lay so still
my husband never discovered me.

Now I drift through the garden,
teaching the trees sleight of hand.
I am shadow, cumulus,
wind over water,
the bird on that branch, only a moment ago.

Milk Valley

They come back at five from the river,
heavy with what has been gathered all day,
our real mothers, hobbling splay-footed through the muck
on their way to the Stygian parlor.
Their eyes, glossy as paperweights, look us over.
We have turned out wrong, all wrong.
They groan and heave themselves inside.
The air takes getting used to. And the flies.
The farmer limps behind, breathing heavily,
shying stones at dawdlers.

Patrolled by skinny cats, they line up,
twitching numbered tags in their ears.
Wire and twine are all that hold the stanchions together
but, truly cowed, no one rebels.
Outside the sky has clabbered. Trees have turned
burnt sienna and raw umber. The barn needs paint.
Along a wooded ridge the farmer's son-in-law
starts home from stalking deer.

Black and white heads bob. They gobble hay.
They agree, winter is coming.
They pray for our souls and for the souls of our enemies
while from their bowels sour pudding spurts into a ditch.
And from their teats the milk of the world
flows through pipes over our heads, splashes, peony-like,
into glass jugs, empties into tanks where paddles
twist and pause, is trundled down the road
to Lewistown, McVeytown, Belleville, up the hill
to the farmer's own table. Tonight we will all drink milk.
The cows will rest and ruminate.
The last train passing through the valley as we fall asleep
will call out, "Mooo- mooo- mooo-ve along."

Summing Up Mr. Cook

The diameter of Mr. Cook's automobile tire is 30 inches. How many revolutions will it make in going 1 mile? If Mr. Cook's car travels 1 mile in 80 seconds, how many revolutions does each wheel make per second? — sixth grade arithmetic problem

Let us begin with Mr. Cook,
who knows the exact diameter of his tires
as well as the number of square feet in his lawn
and how many gallons of paint it takes
to give his house two coats.
He has also figured out (one hates to ask why)
how many cubic feet of air his basement contains—or water.

Mr. Cook likes getting down to the square root of things,
doing his income tax, balancing his checkbook,
calculating his chances. He knows his net worth
and how many shingles cover his roof
with its dormers and intricate cupola.

As a child he counted steps, cracks, posts,
his mother's sighs. These things too are important.
Being ignorant, one suffers.
His favorite game was (still is) BINGO.

Incalculables do not interest Mr. Cook,
who, therefore, cares little for stars,
sparrows, grains of sand or even Mrs. Cook,
who will not measure ingredients
and sometimes loses receipts instead of filing them.

When this happens, Mr. Cook jumps in his car
and drives off, his eyes blinking twice
every three seconds, his heart beating 88 times per minute,
the hairs on his head approaching zero.
He knows how many miles it is to where he's going
and how long it will take. His wheels revolve
precisely so many times, though to the rest of us
they seem to be spinning, just spinning incalculably along.

Big Cars

Jonah had his whale but we had sedans.
Finned and simonized they carried us
through the fifties in their plush bellies,
safer than houses and almost as big.

In school we watched movies about them.
Someday they would float or fly,
or sail themselves on swanroads to the sun.

Boys drew nothing else.
They entered "Cars of Tomorrow" contests,
hoping to win trips to Detroit.

I "learned" on a green Buick
with Hydromatic Drive, which I steered
through a neighbor's hedge.
Behind the wheel even girls were men.

We loved our glossy follies.
They had the power of many horses.
Spellbound we whispered their deathless names—
Cadillac, Oldsmobile, Hudson, Chimera, Leviathan.

Some Gardens

There is, about these apron-sized front yards,
a sassiness that pleases.
Magenta petunias and bright red begonias
jostle each other in rubber tires.
Marigolds bubble from coffee cans
and a yellow rose, rising from rubble,
embroiders a chain link fence.

Behold variety and invention, a sense of making do—
corn mixed with canna lilies,
morning glories rooted in a chipped cup,
a garage wired together by grapevines.
Some yards specialize in one species,
a single season, as if nothing,
having caught hold, can be denied.

Whatever scatters seed or winters over
in dim parlor windows or raises itself perennially up
out of piss and axle grease
through the thick air of maybe a chemical plant
is welcome, seems at home.
The fig tree does not care a fig
for the grime and din of traffic.
In winter, wound with plastic, it still presides
like a crossing guard over the neighborhood.

Driving along on the thruway, we think
we might be content on a stoop
beneath the sunflowers' pensive, bristly heads
or in the shade of castor beans,
keeping company with fiery cockscombs and coleus
and a kitten on a red string.
"Let the world pass," they seem to say.
"You who would hurry by have lost
a chance to be astonished, comforted."

Van Gogh's Bed

is orange,
like Cinderella's coach, like
the sun when he looked it
straight in the eye.

is narrow,
he slept alone, tossing
between two pillows, while it carried him
bumpily to the ball.

is clumsy,
but friendly. A peasant
built the frame; an old wife beat
the mattress till it rose like meringue.

is empty,
morning light pours in
like wine, melody, fragrance,
the memory of happiness.

Checking the Camp

—in memory of James Reynolds (1940–1982)

After he died he went north to the camp for just a little while.
It was October—season of partings. The woods rattled with leaves.
Across the lake a pair of loons, who had carried their young so
    patiently
on their backs through summer, were childless again and could laugh
    about it.

Wind jiggled the dock, which was loose where he had tacked it
    together
in August, hobbling down the steps on a crutch to favor his leg.
Now he could drift without effort wherever he pleased but he couldn't
    fix
anything. Come spring the dock might wash up on another beach
and have to be replaced. He checked the pipes and wondered if anyone
would think to kick the pump sometimes. Probably would when it
    stopped.

Since the doors were locked he went down the chimney. Mice didn't
    run
from him anymore but kept on nibbling a greasy box of matches.
Ordinarily he would have built a fire. If Amy and Linda and Lily,
the fat Newfoundland, had been around there would have been
    something cooking.

Likely Amy'd be playing store in the spare room. He thought of them
fondly, as if he were watching a jerky home movie in which they took
    off
in the red canoe. Amy was chattering. Linda was paddling with swift,
firm strokes, while Lily crouched in the stern, ready to save them.
It was all right; they'd manage. The camp would be there when they
    got back.

Narcissus in Mid-December

Narcissus, as light recedes and the year,
growing febrile, revels in its loss,
you, trailing green ribbons, bring us
a gift of fragrant snow.

Who can say what we hoped for?
We would have settled for spring again,
those baskets of bloom, those pink cloudy candies,
buds breaking like glass balls to show us
our funny selves, looking back laughing.

Instead, Narcissus, you give us
the heart bathed in its own exuberant fountain.
Have you no message?
Only this eager blossoming?

Even while we sleep and the household sleeps—
animals, furniture, crumbs by the
kitchen door—Narcissus,
you stand watch, mute and dreamless
during your one brief season,
as if unwilling to miss, for even an instant, Being,
the Whole that embraces us.

We wake and move between this and that
in the glow of your doomed, waxy stars.
Lessen our solitude, Sister,
the hand stretched forth, serene
novitiate from the ancient, ineffable garden.

Domesticity

1. Nesting Robins

As if for our instruction they begin
to build it in the bushes at the edge
of the back deck. Crouched on a rail, even
the cat takes lessons: twigs from hemlock hedges,

thready roots and weeds, pieces of string.
"You see," they seem to say, "what can be made
of all you throw away." The gatherings—
detritus of our lives—cleverly laid

in shady notch, a wild corsage. And now
mud from the garden, mixed with humus, air-
lifted to the site and smoothed in place

with dusty breasts. (The birdbath is a wallow,
all those rinsing-offs!) A swatch of hair
and it's done—already sagging at the base.

2. *Eggs*

No greeting card, this small, fierce, brooding bird,
still as the milk glass hen upon glass nest
that fills at Eastertide. Last night we heard
a ruckus in the garden—what foul pest

is out there? Steve and I get up to check
and find the bird still sitting tight, cruel
beak in silhouette. All's well. The deck
is clear. So back to our own dreamy vigil.

Spring's been rainy, windy, cold. The birds take
turns on duty, ride the storms, fill up
on earthworms. Each child must be raised to see

these blue beginnings, ancient thrifty shapes,
four throbbing drops in an odd cup
under the glittering eye, the homely eaves.

3. The Young

Why not just walk (hop, as it were, fly) out
on this unsavory mass of squirming flesh,
more active day by day, nothing but spouts
down which is poured regurgitated mess?

Kate tries to help, puts raisins within reach;
nothing will do but worms. The adults shove
each other off the nest as if competing
for most self-sacrificing. "It's not love,"

we tell the children, having reserved that
for ourselves, "It's instinct." Bugaboos arise:
a jay dive-bombs the nest, the cat blunders

by, regrets it. Now when the brood is sat
upon three heads stick out. Their feeble cries
increase, *peep, peep,* as we drift toward summer.

4. *Flight*

Somehow they got out, flapped (one can't say *flew*).
Under their pinfeather cloaks they're baby
Superbirds, chirping and scrabbling through
the underbrush. This is progress, maybe.

One hops on a twig from the Christmas tree,
stops, teeters, then preens. A trick like any
other. Icarus opens wide, goes *peep*
and gets a snack. We walk the cat. Many

more stages? We're tired of all these fluttering
hearts (including ours) and wings, these squawky
pulltoys. What a noisy life: *peep, peep,*

Ben's fireworks, Kate's Haydn. . . . Hedge and gutter
pipe, "Hooray!" ("Hurry!") Finally a gawky
speckled shadow wobbles between two trees.

5. *And After*

Today three robins come to the back yard;
two of them sport soft burnt orange breasts,
one's mottled still. The latter pecks, not hard,
then twitters, head tossed back, its body pressed

to the grass, trying to seem small. Sometimes
the ploy succeeds—one of the others dumps
something in. But nobody's fooled. It's time
for Junior to be off. The grown-ups jump

about flirtatiously. Their old nest still
looks just the same. A derelict askew
among fat rhododendron pods, it sways

in the hot breeze. They might come back, but Nell
says they won't. She's seen them building a new
nest in the sweet gum over the driveway.

Anatomy Theater: 1945

"For every thing that lives is Holy." — *William Blake*

In the cellar Mother is gutting a hen
as if she were rearranging her pocketbook.
Here come the gizzard, the liver, the heavy heart.
She holds them out like chocolate-covered cherries.
Here come the plump, airy lights, the craw—
she slits it to show me pebbles and corn, mixed
small change—and see, see here!
She shakes her hen-bag and lifts out a handful of gold
costume jewelry, the kind my aunts keep
getting rid of by giving it to me: eggs
which in time the hen would have laid,
had she not lost her head, had she kept her wits about her.
Perhaps Mother has told me . . . perhaps
she has not yet told me
all that we must know about ourselves. In any case,
I am aware of my own need to be filled and emptied.

The blood of the hen drips from Mother's hands
into a bucket of hot water, spreads, and vanishes
as my face waxes and wanes. Meanwhile
there seems no end of orbs being plucked from the hen's
raw side, though each is smaller than the last, and no end
to the meals we will make of them,
swirling through thick, pale gravy.
No end to flesh and the cutting edge and what will flow,
to night and day, biting each other's tails,
to the seasons following meekly in order,
singing "Jesus Loves Me."

Mother dips the hen and strips her, singeing
the skin with matches, pushing out pin feathers.
Above us rises a stage, forever set in the forties,
with genuine brick linoleum, sunny sheers,
a stove that almost prances on thin, white legs,

and walls which open to show the world
what I must imagine, as my parents,
in startling undress, turn to each other again and again,
after my eyes unwillingly close. Over all
dust drifts endlessly, and is endlessly gathered up
and cast away. And there is no end in sight
to the shining strangeness of everything.

About the Author

Jane Flanders was born in Waynesboro, Pennsylvania, in 1940. She was educated at Bryn Mawr College, where she studied musicology, and at Columbia University, where she studied English literature. She is the author of two previously published collections of poetry: *Leaving and Coming Back* and *The Students of Snow,* which won the Juniper Prize in 1982. Among her awards are poetry fellowships from the National Endowment for the Arts and the New York Foundation for the Arts. She lives in Pelham, New York.

PITT POETRY SERIES

Ed Ochester, General Editor

Dannie Abse, *Collected Poems*
Claribel Alegría, *Flowers from the Volcano*
Jon Anderson, *Death and Friends*
Jon Anderson, *In Sepia*
Jon Anderson, *Looking for Jonathan*
Maggie Anderson, *Cold Comfort*
Michael Benedikt, *The Badminton at Great Barrington; Or, Gustave Mahler
   & the Chattanooga Choo-Choo*
Michael Burkard, *Ruby for Grief*
Kathy Callaway, *Heart of the Garfish*
Siv Cedering, *Letters from the Floating World*
Lorna Dee Cervantes, *Emplumada*
Robert Coles, *A Festering Sweetness: Poems of American People*
Kate Daniels, *The White Wave*
Norman Dubie, *Alehouse Sonnets*
Stuart Dybek, *Brass Knuckles*
Odysseus Elytis, *The Axion Esti*
Jane Flanders, *Timepiece*
Brendan Galvin, *The Minutes No One Owns*
Gary Gildner, *Blue Like the Heavens: New & Selected Poems*
Bruce Guernsey, *January Thaw*
Michael S. Harper, *Song: I Want a Witness*
Barbara Helfgott Hyett, *In Evidence: Poems of the Liberation of Nazi
   Concentration Camps*
Milne Holton and Paul Vangelisti, eds., *The New Polish Poetry: A Bilingual
   Collection*
David Huddle, *Paper Boy*
Phyllis Janowitz, *Temporary Dwellings*
Lawrence Joseph, *Curriculum Vitae*
Lawrence Joseph, *Shouting at No One*
Shirley Kaufman, *From One Life to Another*
Shirley Kaufman, *Gold Country*
Etheridge Knight, *The Essential Etheridge Knight*
Ted Kooser, *One World at a Time*
Ted Kooser, *Sure Signs: New and Selected Poems*
Larry Levis, *Winter Stars*
Larry Levis, *Wrecking Crew*
Robert Louthan, *Living in Code*
Tom Lowenstein, tr., *Eskimo Poems from Canada and Greenland*